JUICING FOR BEGIN

Enjoy These 1600 Days Of Quick And Tasty Recipes, Perfect For Those Who Are Short On Time But Want To Stay Fit And Have A Healthy Life

MATT BLACK

DISCLAIMER: THIS BOOK DOES NOT PROVIDE MEDICAL ADVICE

This book contains information for general guidance only, including, but not limited to, written content, images, photos, and other items. Nothing in this book is meant to be a replacement for qualified medical guidance, diagnosis, or treatment. Never dismiss expert medical advice or put off getting it because of something you have read on this book; instead, always seek it out right away if you have any questions about a medical condition or treatment from your doctor or another trained healthcare practitioner. The reader is alone in charge of their actions.

Why should I read this particular book?

Welcome, dear reader, to a journey of transformation, a journey that begins with the simplest of ingredients and ends with a healthier, more vibrant you. You may be wondering, "Why should I choose this book about juicing over the countless others that line the shelves?" The answer is simple: this book is not just about juicing; it's about you.

This is not a book that merely tells you how to juice. It's a book that understands you, your busy schedule, your desire to live a healthier life, and your need for clear, simple, and effective guidance. It's a book that respects your individuality, your unique health goals, and your personal taste preferences. In the pages that follow, you won't find a one-size-fits-all approach. Instead, you'll discover a wealth of knowledge tailored to your specific needs, whether you're a busy parent looking for quick and nutritious recipes your kids will love, a health-conscious professional seeking to boost your energy levels, or a beginner just starting your journey into the world of juicing.

This book is the result of extensive research, countless hours of experimentation, and a deep passion for health and wellness. It's a book that cuts through the noise and offers you the truth about juicing, debunking common myths and providing you with the facts you need to make informed decisions about your health.

But more than anything, this is a book that empowers you. It gives you the tools, the knowledge, and the confidence to take control of your health, one delicious glass of juice at a time. It's a book that inspires you to explore, to experiment, and to discover the incredible power of fruits and vegetables.

So why choose this book? Because this book chooses you. It understands you. It empowers you. And it's ready to guide you on your journey to a healthier, happier life.

Welcome to your juicing journey. Let's begin!

--- INDEX ---

Why should I read this particular book? 3
Knowing The Basics Of Juice 9
The Real Benefits of Juices 10
Peculiarities Of All Types Of Juices 11
Juice Extraction Methods and Types of Juicers 13
The Symphony Of Colours 13
Vitamins, what they are, why they are essential 15
10 Tips To Get An Amazing Juice 16
10 Tips For Staying Motivated And For Making It A Sustainable Habit 18
10 Tips How Involve The Family And Kids 20
Making Your Own Fresh Juice at Home 22

WEIGTH LOSS 27

Slimming Citrus Green 27
Green Detox Elixir With Kale 28
Berry Blast 28
Tropical Delight 29
Beetroot Boost 30
Citrus Zing 30
Refreshing Cucumber Lime 31
Green Goddess 32
Pineapple Ginger Twist 32
Apple Carrot Glow 33
Green Detox Cleanse 34
Berry Blast Slimmer 35
Cucumber Lime Refresher 35
Carrot Ginger Zing 36
Watermelon Mint Splash 37
Pineapple Kale Kick 37

Grapefruit Detox Delight 38
Beet Berry Blast 39
Apple Celery Slimmer 39
Pineapple Spinach Slim Down 40
Green Detox Elixir With Spinach 41
Beet Detox Power 42
Citrus Detox Zing 42
Pineapple Ginger Cleanse 43
Ginger Turmeric Cleanse 43
Papaya Pineapple Detox 44
Watermelon Cucumber Cooler 45
Carrot Orange Detoxifier 46
Minty Berry Cleanse 46

DETOX 48

Revitalizing Green Cleanse 48
Citrus Detox Blast 49
Beetroot Power Cleanse 49
Berry Antioxidant Detox Blend 50
Green Ginger Detox Elixir 51
Pineapple Mint Detox Refresher 52
Carrot Turmeric Cleansing Elixir 52
Refreshing Green Detox Delight 53
Cabbage Cleansing Elixir 54
Watermelon Mint Detox Splash 55
Vitamin C Power Boost 55
Antioxidant Berry Boost 57
Spicy Immune Kick 58
Carrot Citrus Boost 58
Tropical Immunity Tonic 59
Zesty Green Apple Boost 60
Mango Carrot Immunity Blend 60
Red Bell Pepper Vitality 61
Refreshing Melon Cooler 62

INCREASE ENERGY AND VITALITY 63

Supercharged Green Energy 63

Refreshing Citrus Burst 64

Berry Power Boost 64

Tropical Energy Refresher 65

Zesty Green Revitalizer 66

Carrot Ginger Power Boost 66

Tropical Coconut Energizer 67

Refreshing Watermelon Revive 68

Pineapple Kale Power Punch 68

Beetroot Citrus Energizer 69

Energizing Green Power 70

Tropical Energy Boost 71

Refreshing Beet Berry Burst 72

Citrus Carrot Recharge 72

Green Power Punch 73

Minty Pineapple Boost 74

Berry Blast Energizer 75

DIGESTIVE PROCESS 76

Leafy Green Digestive Cleanser 76

Tropical Digestive Soother 77

Carrot Ginger Digestive Tonic 77

Cooling Digestive Refresher 78

Apple Celery Digestive Cleanse 79

Ginger Turmeric Digestive Tonic 79

Papaya Mint Digestive Refresher 80

Pineapple Ginger Digestive Aid 81

Beetroot Carrot Digestive Booster 81

Green Apple Aloe Digestive Soother 82

Ginger Lemon Detox 83

Pineapple Mint Cooler 84

Green Detox Delight 84

Beetroot Carrot Cleanse 85

Papaya Digestive Soother 86

Cucumber Celery Refresher 86
Mango Ginger Cleanse 87
Carrot Apple Refresher 88
Watermelon Basil Cleanse 89
Pear Spinach Cleanse 89

HEART HEALTH 91

Berry Heart Booster With Orange 91
Beetroot Apple Elixir 91
Citrus Kale Cleanse 92
Pomegranate Beet Blend 93
Green Apple Spinach Delight 93
Carrot Ginger Splash 94
Turmeric Pineapple Punch 95
Spinach Avocado Heart Boost 96
Celery Cucumber Cooler 96
Apple Beet Detox 97
Ginger Orange Zing 98
Kiwi Berry Delight 98
Cucumber Mint Refresher 99
Spinach Grapefruit Twist 100
Mango Carrot Smoothie 100
Berry Heart Booster with Pomegranate 101
Citrus Beet Power 102
Apple Celery Refresher 102
Spinach Tomato Elixir 103
Grapefruit Ginger Zing 104
Carrot Orange Antioxidant 104
Turmeric Pineapple Twist 105
Papaya Mango Delight 106
Cranberry Apple Fusion 106
Watermelon Basil Crush 107
Citrus Immune Kick 108
Turmeric Carrot Booster 109
Berry Immunity Blast 109
Ginger Beet Elixir 110

Green Immunity Boost 111
Pineapple Ginger Immune Boost 112
Orange Carrot Sunshine 112
Strawberry Kiwi Boost 113
Cranberry Apple Defense 114
Melon Mint Immune Refresher 114
Ginger Carrot Sunrise 115
Turmeric Mango Sunrise 116
Coconut Water Citrus Splash 117

RECEIPES FOR KIDS 118

Orange Strawberry Delight 118
Apple Carrot Crush 118
Tropical Paradise 119
Very Berry Blast 120
Green Lemonade 120
Cucumber Mint Cooler 121
Watermelon Lime Quencher 122
Pineapple Mango Punch 122
Carrot Orange Sip 123
Pineapple Kiwi Splash 123

CONCLUSION 125

BONUS 127

1) HIIT Exercises 127
2) Free E-Book: Copycat Recipes By Matt Black 128
3) 10 SMOOTHIES RECIPES 129

Knowing The Basics Of Juice

Ah, the humble juice, a symphony of flavors captured in a glass, a vibrant elixir that whispers the secrets of nature's bounty. But what is it that transforms a simple piece of fruit or a humble vegetable into this life-giving nectar? Let's unravel this mystery together. At its heart, juicing is the process of extracting the liquid from fruits and vegetables, leaving behind the solid fibrous material. But it's so much more than that. It's an art, a science, a dance of balance and harmony. It's about understanding the unique properties of each ingredient, the sweet tang of an apple, the earthy richness of a beet, the refreshing crispness of a cucumber. It's about knowing how to combine these flavors to create a juice that not only nourishes your body but also delights your palate. But most importantly, it's about embracing the idea that health and pleasure are not mutually exclusive, that something as nutritious as a glass of juice can also be a source of immense joy. So, let's embark on this journey of discovery together, exploring the wonderful world of juices, one sip at a time.

The Real Benefits of Juices

Imagine, dear reader, a cascade of vitality flowing into your body with each sip, a river of wellness that nourishes, heals, and rejuvenates. This is the true power of juices. These vibrant elixirs are more than just a delightful blend of flavors; they are a concentrated source of the essential vitamins, minerals, and antioxidants that our bodies crave. Each glass of juice is a love letter from nature, a potent reminder of the healing power of the earth's bounty.

When we consume juices, we are inviting wellness into our lives. We are boosting our immunity, enhancing our digestion, and infusing our bodies with energy. We are cleansing our systems, promoting healthier skin, and even supporting our heart health. But the benefits of juicing extend beyond the physical. The simple act of juicing invites mindfulness into our daily routine, encouraging us to slow down, to savor the moment, to connect with the food we consume. The benefits of consuming juices are numerous and far-reaching, encompassing various aspects of our health and well-being. In a world where our modern lifestyles often fall short in providing the necessary nutrients, juices emerge as a potent ally, delivering a concentrated dose of essential vitamins, minerals, and antioxidants. These vibrant elixirs offer a convenient and efficient way to supplement our diets with the vital components our bodies require for optimal functioning.

One of the primary advantages of incorporating juices into our routine is their potential to boost our immune system. Packed with immune-supporting nutrients such as vitamin C and antioxidants, juices can fortify our body's natural defense mechanisms, helping to ward off infections and promote overall wellness. Additionally, juices are renowned for their role in enhancing digestion. The inherent enzymes present in freshly squeezed juices assist in breaking down food, facilitating nutrient absorption and promoting a healthy digestive process. The fiber content in certain juices also aids in regulating bowel movements and supporting gastrointestinal health.

Moreover, juices are often celebrated for their ability to invigorate and revitalize our energy levels. By providing a direct source of easily assimilated nutrients, juices offer a natural pick-me-up, replenishing vital vitamins and minerals and contributing to a sustained feeling of vitality throughout the day. In the realm of skincare, the benefits of juices shine through as well. The abundance of antioxidants found in many fruits and vegetables can help combat oxidative stress, reducing the signs of aging and promoting a radiant complexion from within.

Furthermore, juicing has shown potential benefits for heart health. Certain juices, such as beet juice, have been associated with supporting healthy blood pressure levels and promoting cardiovascular well-being. Their rich nutrient profiles, including potassium and nitric oxide, can contribute to a healthy cardiovascular system.

Beyond the physical advantages, the act of juicing promotes a deeper connection with our dietary choices. It encourages mindfulness, inviting us to appreciate the flavors, textures, and vibrant colors of the ingredients we select. This mindful approach to nourishment can cultivate a sense of gratitude and awareness, fostering a harmonious relationship between our bodies and the nourishing power of nature.

In summary, the benefits of juices extend to multiple facets of our health. From bolstering our immune system and aiding digestion to energizing our bodies and enhancing our skin's radiance, juices offer a natural and convenient means of fortifying our well-being. Embracing the practice of juicing can empower us to proactively support our health, providing a foundation for vitality and longevity.

Peculiarities Of All Types Of Juices

Weight Loss Juices: These juices are typically low in calories and high in fiber, which can help you feel full and satisfied without consuming a lot of calories. They often include ingredients like celery, cucumber, kale, spinach, and green apples, which are low in sugar and high in nutrients. Some weight loss juices may also include ingredients like ginger or cayenne pepper, which are thought to boost metabolism.

Detox Juices: Detox juices are designed to cleanse the body and improve overall health. They often include ingredients that are high in antioxidants and have natural detoxifying properties, such as beets, lemons, carrots, and turmeric. These juices are often rich in vitamins and minerals and are intended to support the body's natural detoxification processes.

Energy and Vitality Juices: These juices are typically high in vitamins and minerals that are known to boost energy levels, such as B-vitamins and iron. They often include ingredients like oranges, strawberries, bananas, and spinach. These juices are also usually high in natural sugars, which can provide a quick source of energy.

Digestive Health Juices: These juices often include ingredients that are known to support digestive health, such as ginger, mint, and fennel. They may also include fruits and vegetables that are high in dietary fiber, like apples and pears, which can help promote regular bowel movements and overall digestive health.

Heart Health Juices: Heart health juices are typically high in ingredients that are known to support cardiovascular health. This includes fruits and vegetables that are high in heart-healthy nutrients like potassium, flavonoids, and antioxidants. Common ingredients include oranges, bananas, berries, and beets. These juices may also be low in sodium and high in dietary fiber, which is beneficial for heart health.

Immunity Boost Juices: Immunity boost juices are packed with ingredients high in vitamin C, antioxidants, and other nutrients known to support the immune system. Common ingredients include oranges, lemons, grapefruit, ginger, and turmeric. These juices are designed to help protect the body against illness and disease.

Juice Extraction Methods and Types of Juicers

Juice can be extracted from fruits and vegetables in a number of different ways, each with its own set of pros and cons. In this section, we'll take a look at the most popular approaches, as well as the different kinds of juicers that can be purchased.

The pulp can be juiced by spinning it in a centrifuge to separate the juice. Produce juice is extracted by cutting the fruit or vegetable into little bits and then pressing the pieces against a fine mesh filter. Centrifugal juicers are quick and easy to use, however the juice they produce may be less nutrient-dense than that extracted using traditional methods.

With mastication (also known as cold extraction), the fruit or vegetable is crushed by an auger or gear before being forced through a filter. Masticating juicers are more expensive, take longer to prepare and clean, and yield thinner juice due to increased oxidation.

Juice extractors: thanks to their ability to use a cold extraction procedure, they keep all the fruit's beneficial nutrients and enzymes intact while getting the most juice out of the fruit. Vitamins, minerals, and living enzymes, all of which are vital to good health, can be replenished by drinking cold-pressed juices.

In conclusion, you should select a process for extracting juice and a juicer that works best for your needs, your budget, and your tastes. There is a juicer for everyone, whether they want a quick and easy way to prepare juice or the maximum nutritional benefit from their juice. Juices from fruits and vegetables should be included in a healthy diet rather than serving as a sole source of nutrition.

The Symphony Of Colours

Each vegetable and fruit color reveals a distinct symphony of nutrients that nourish our bodies and spark our senses in nature's bountiful harvest. Let's explore nature's beautiful colors and their amazing benefits.

White: Cauliflower's delicate florets and the onion's layered brilliance demonstrate white's beauty. Sulfur molecules in these jewels aid detoxification and immunological function. White fruits like pears include vitamin C and fiber, which aid digestion and immunity.

Red: Red's striking intensity seduces us. Tomatoes, strawberries, and red bell peppers fill our plates. These red gems boost heart health, fight oxidative stress, and improve well-being thanks to lycopene and anthocyanins. Red fruits and vegetables also include vitamin C, which boosts collagen formation and immunity.

Yellow and Orange: Yellow and orange add warmth and liveliness to our cuisine. Oranges and lemons boost collagen development and immunity with vitamin C. Beta-carotene, a precursor to vitamin A that improves eye health and protection, is found in mangoes and carrots.

Purple: Purple's richness captivates us. Eggplants, blueberries, and purple cabbage dazzle with their color. These jewels include anthocyanins, powerful antioxidants with anti-inflammatory and brain-health benefits. Purple produce contains vitamins A and C, which boosts health.

Black: Wonders lie in the dark. Blackberries' velvety richness and black beans' enigmatic charm reveal black's beauty. Antioxidants, fiber, and minerals help digestion, cardiovascular health, and vitality in these gems.

Vegetable and fruit hues are beautiful and a tribute to nature's bounty. Phytonutrients and antioxidants in each color boost health. This vivid palette opens up a world of flavors and health advantages, improving our lives and enjoying nature's richness. Let's enjoy nature's rainbow and its health benefits.

Vitamins, what they are, why they are essential

Vitamins are the unseen heroes of our bodies, necessary for appropriate cell function and growth. They are like puzzle pieces that, when fitted together, form a comprehensive picture of health and vigor.

Vitamins A, C, D, E, K, and the B-complex vitamins are among the 13 important vitamins. These vitamins are classified as either fat-soluble (A, D, E, K) or water-soluble (C and B vitamins). Each vitamin has a distinct purpose. Vitamin A, for example, helps to preserve teeth, bones, and skin, whereas vitamin C is a potent antioxidant that assists iron absorption and tissue health.

But where do these vitamins originate? The explanation is straightforward: it comes from the food we eat. A varied diet rich in fruits, vegetables, dairy, legumes, lentils, and whole grains offers the required vitamins. Vitamin A, for example, is contained in animal-based meals such as liver and fish, as well as fruits and vegetables such as carrots and spinach.

Taking vitamins is essential for humans. Without them, our bodies would be unable to accomplish important processes such as energy production, red blood cell synthesis, immune system modulation, and much more. Furthermore, a vitamin shortage can cause weariness, weakness, skin and hair problems, and, in certain situations, more serious disorders.

Finally, vitamins play an important role in keeping our bodies healthy and robust. They are the lifeblood that powers every cell, organ, and function in our bodies. Let us ensure that our bodies receive the vitamins they require to thrive. Remember that your health is your most valuable possession. Take good care of it.

10 Tips To Get An Amazing Juice

Unlocking the full potential of amazing juices is within your grasp. Here are a few practical tips to help you embark on a journey of creating and enjoying tantalizing, nutrient-rich juices:

1. Choose Fresh, Quality Produce: Selecting fresh and high-quality fruits and vegetables is crucial for vibrant and flavorful juices. Opt for ripe produce that feels firm and looks vibrant, with no signs of spoilage or wilting.

2. Variety is Key: Embrace a diverse array of fruits and vegetables to create well-rounded juices. Different ingredients offer a wide spectrum of nutrients and flavors, ensuring a nutrient-packed and delightful experience. Experiment with seasonal produce to add variety to your juicing repertoire.

3. Preparation Matters: Properly wash and clean your produce before juicing to remove any dirt, bacteria, or pesticides. Remove any tough skin, seeds, or pits from fruits, and trim away any wilted or damaged portions of vegetables.

4. Balance Sweetness and Greens: Strike a harmonious balance between sweet and green ingredients in your juice recipes. While fruits bring natural sweetness, incorporating leafy greens like spinach or kale adds essential vitamins, minerals, and a nutritional boost without overpowering the flavors.

5. Add a Citrus Kick: Citrus fruits, such as oranges, lemons, or limes, add a refreshing zing to your juices. Their tangy flavor helps cut through the richness of other ingredients while providing a dose of vitamin C and brightness to your concoctions.

6. Don't Forget the Fiber: Consider using a blender or masticating juicer that retains some fiber in your juices. While extracting pure juice can offer a more concentrated nutrient profile, incorporating a bit of fiber can aid digestion and help maintain a balanced diet.

7. Sip Mindfully and Hydrate: Treat your juice as a moment of self-care. Sip it slowly, savoring the flavors and allowing your body to fully absorb the nutrients. Remember that juices can be hydrating but may not replace the need for regular water intake.

8. Keep It Fresh: Juices are best enjoyed immediately after juicing to maximize freshness and nutrient content. However, if you need to store your juice, do so in an airtight container in the refrigerator for no longer than 24-48 hours to maintain optimal quality.

9. Get Creative with Additions: Don't be afraid to experiment with herbs, spices, or superfood boosters to enhance your juices. Fresh mint, ginger, turmeric, or a sprinkle of chia seeds can elevate the flavor profile and add an extra nutritional punch.

10. Listen to Your Body: Everyone's taste preferences and nutritional needs are unique. Pay attention to how different ingredients make you feel and adjust recipes accordingly. Let your body guide you towards the combinations that truly nourish and delight you.

With these practical tips in hand, you're well on your way to creating amazing juices that tantalize your taste buds and provide a burst of nourishment for your body. So, embrace the art of juicing, let your creativity flow, and enjoy the vibrant world of flavors and health benefits that awaits you.

10 Tips For Staying Motivated And For Making It A Sustainable Habit

Staying motivated and making juicing a routine can help you enjoy long-term advantages. Here are some pointers to help you stay motivated and include juicing into your daily routine:

1. Set Realistic Goals: Begin your juicing adventure by creating realistic and attainable goals. Having precise goals, whether it's juicing a certain number of times per week or adding specific fruits and veggies into your dishes, will give you a feeling of purpose and direction.

2. Establish a habit: Create a consistent juicing habit that fits into your everyday schedule. Set up specific times or days for juicing to make it a regular part of your routine. Having a schedule can help you make juicing a habit and keep you on track.

3. Keep it Simple: Avoid intricate recipes or lengthy ingredient lists. Begin with simple juice combinations you appreciate and gradually introduce other flavors and ingredients. Juicing will be more approachable and sustainable in the long run if you keep it simple.

4. Plan and Prep Ahead: Planning your juicing sessions ahead of time can help you save time and ensuring you have all of the necessary components on hand. Consider chopping and storing fruits and vegetables in batches to speed up the juicing process.

5. Find Inspiration: Look for ideas in recipe books, online resources, or juicing-related social media communities. Investigate new taste combinations, read success stories, and connect with people who share your juicing enthusiasm. Being surrounded by positive influences might help you stay motivated and inspired.

6. Track Your Progress: Keep a notebook or use a tracking tool to keep track of your juicing experiences, recipes, and how you feel after drinking various combinations. Keeping track of your progress allows you to reflect on your journey, celebrate your accomplishments, and find patterns that work best for you.

7. appreciate Small Wins: Recognize and appreciate your small victories along the way. Whether it's finishing a week of consistent juicing or including a new produce into your recipe, modest victories build momentum and strengthen your commitment to the practice.

8. Experiment and Have Fun: In your juicing adventure, embrace the spirit of discovery and experimentation. Experiment with various fruits, veggies, and flavor combinations. Consider juicing an opportunity to broaden your culinary horizons and explore new, wholesome recipes.

9. Accountability and Support: Discuss your juicing goals with a friend or family member, or join an online group that gives accountability and support. Having someone to share your progress, exchange ideas, and offer encouragement might help you stay motivated.

10. Listen to Your Body: Notice how your body reacts to juicing. Take note of any good changes, such as more energy, better digestion, or a general sense of well-being. This awareness will help you remember the benefits of juicing and stay dedicated to the habit.

By implementing these juicing techniques into your routine, you will not only stay motivated, but you will also develop a sustainable habit that will become a vital part of your healthy lifestyle. Remember that juicing is a personal experience, so tailor these guidelines to your preferences to make it a fun and sustainable habit over time.

10 Tips How Involve The Family And Kids

Involving the family and children in the preparation of juices may be a fun and engaging method to establish healthy habits and make great memories together. Here are some ideas for making juicing a family affair:

1. Educate and Explain: Teach your family, particularly your children, about the advantages of fruits and vegetables and how juicing can help you live a healthier lifestyle. Explain the significance of eating a diversity of colors and flavors for general health.

2. Make it a Group Project: Encourage the entire family to take part in the juicing process. Assign age-appropriate tasks to your children, such as washing produce, peeling fruits, or operating the juicer. In order to make delicious and nutritious juices, emphasize the necessity of collaboration and teamwork.

3. Be Creative with Recipes: Involve your family, including youngsters, in recipe selection and juice creation. Allow children to try various fruits, veggies, and flavors. This encourages creativity and allows individuals to take charge of their healthy lifestyle choices.

4. Start a Family Garden: Start a modest family garden or grow herbs indoors. Plant, nurture, and harvest fruits and vegetables with your children. Using homegrown vegetables in your juices gives you a sense of success as well as a stronger connection to nature.

5. Make it Colorful and Fun: During the juicing process, emphasize the brilliant colors of fruits and vegetables. Allow your children to choose colorful ingredients and make aesthetically interesting juices. Encourage children to name their creations to generate enthusiasm and ingenuity.

6. Taste Testing and Flavors: Encourage family members, particularly children, to taste new juices and share their thoughts. Make a taste-testing activity in which everyone scores the flavors or tries to guess the components. This broadens their palate and makes juicing more participatory and pleasurable.

7. Celebrate Achievements: As a family, celebrate milestones and achievements. Recognize and reward attempts to incorporate healthful juices into regular routines. This positive reinforcement stimulates children and emphasizes the significance of making healthy choices.

8. Educational Resources: Look for books, films, or documentaries for children that promote healthy eating and juicing. Involve your family in learning about nutrition, the advantages of fruits and vegetables, and the interesting information about various foods.

9. Set a Good Example: Set a good example by frequently drinking juice and expressing your enthusiasm for healthy choices. Children are more likely to adopt healthy habits if they observe their parents and caregivers doing so on a regular basis.

10. Have Fun and Enjoy the Process: Remember that getting the family involved in juicing is about more than just the final product; it's about the delight of spending quality time together. Play music, share laughter, and create a nice ambiance in the kitchen to make juicing more enjoyable.

You may foster a shared appreciation for healthy behaviors and create a supportive environment for choosing nutritious choices by involving the family and children in the preparation of juices. The event becomes a treasured bonding time, strengthening both your body and your family's bonds.

Making Your Own Fresh Juice at Home

Juicing is an excellent method to incorporate more fruits and vegetables into your diet, and it provides numerous health benefits such as immune system support, detoxification help, and weight reduction assistance. But the best thing is... With a few simple ingredients and techniques, you can make delicious, nutritious juices right in your own kitchen.

Step 1: Select Your Ingredients

The first step in making your own juice is selecting the components. Consider the nutritional value, flavor, and how they will blend together when choosing fruits and vegetables. Include a range of colors and flavors to create a well-balanced juice. Choose a sweet fruit such as apple or pineapple, a green vegetable such as spinach or kale, and a root vegetable such as carrot or beetroot. Don't forget to add some citrus, such lemon or lime, for a refreshing tang and to help preserve the juice.

Step 2: Get Your Ingredients Ready

After you've decided on your ingredients, it's time to get them ready for juicing. To eliminate any dirt or pesticides, properly wash all fruits and vegetables. You may leave the peels on organic veggies for added nutrients and fiber. Non-organic food, on the other hand, should be peeled to avoid pesticide residue. Cut your ingredients into small enough bits to fit through your juicer.

Step 3: Juice the Ingredients

Now for the exciting part: juicing! The process may differ significantly depending on the type of juicer you have (centrifugal, masticating, or triturating). In general, you will feed your prepared fruits and vegetables into the juicer, which will extract the juice while separating the pulp. Remember to juice slowly to keep the nutrients and enzymes in your vegetables intact.

Step 4: Sip Your Juice

It's time to savor the fruits (and vegetables) of your labor once you've juiced all of your components. Fresh juice is best consumed right away because it begins to lose nutrients as soon as it is produced. If you must store your juice, keep it in an airtight container in the refrigerator and drink it within 24 hours.

Making your own juice at home is an easy and enjoyable process. You can have a fresh, nutritious beverage personalized to your tastes and health needs with just a few ingredients and a little time. Why not give it a shot? Have fun juicing!

RECIPES

WEIGTH LOSS

Slimming Citrus Green

Ingredients:

- 2 large oranges
- 1 medium-sized grapefruit
- 1 cup spinach leaves
- 1/2 cucumber
- 1 small apple
- 1/2 inch ginger root (optional for added flavor)

Procedure:

1. Peel the oranges and grapefruit, removing any seeds or pith. Cut them into segments.
2. Wash the spinach leaves thoroughly and remove any tough stems.
3. Slice the cucumber and apple into chunks, ensuring they are small enough to fit through the juicer.
4. If using ginger, peel the skin and cut it into small pieces.
5. Add all the prepared ingredients into a juicer and extract the juice.
6. Once the juice is ready, stir it gently to combine the flavors.
7. Pour the juice into a glass and serve chilled.

Calories: 120

Sugar: 12 g

Green Detox Elixir With Kale

Ingredients:

- 2 cups kale
- 1 medium cucumber
- 1 green apple
- 1 lemon (peeled)
- 1-inch piece of ginger

Procedure:

1. Wash the kale leaves thoroughly and remove any tough stems.
2. Slice the cucumber and green apple into chunks.
3. Peel the lemon.
4. Peel and chop the ginger.
5. Add all the ingredients to a juicer and extract the juice.
6. Stir the juice gently and serve chilled.

Calories: 110

Sugar: 10 g

Berry Blast

Ingredients:

- 1 cup strawberries
- 1 cup blueberries

- 1 cup raspberries
- 1 medium orange (peeled)

Procedure:

1. Wash the berries.
2. Peel the orange.
3. Add all the ingredients to a juicer and extract the juice.
4. Stir the juice gently and serve chilled.

Calories: 150

Sugar: 20 g

Tropical Delight

Ingredients:

- 1 cup pineapple chunks
- 1 medium mango (peeled and pitted)
- 1 medium orange (peeled)
- 1 medium carrot

Procedure:

1. Slice the pineapple, mango, and orange into chunks.
2. Wash and chop the carrot.
3. Add all the ingredients to a juicer and extract the juice.

4. Stir the juice gently and serve chilled.

Calories: 170

Sugar: 30 g

Beetroot Boost

Ingredients:

- 1 medium beetroot (peeled)
- 2 medium carrots
- 1 medium apple
- 1-inch piece of ginger

Procedure:

1. Wash and chop the beetroot, carrots, and apple into chunks.
2. Peel and chop the ginger.
3. Add all the ingredients to a juicer and extract the juice.
4. Stir the juice gently and serve chilled.

Calories: 160

Sugar: 20 g

Citrus Zing

Ingredients:

- 2 medium oranges (peeled)

- 1 medium grapefruit (peeled)

- 1 medium lemon (peeled)

Procedure:

1. Peel the oranges, grapefruit, and lemon.

2. Add all the ingredients to a juicer and extract the juice.

3. Stir the juice gently and serve chilled.

Calories: 100

Sugar: 15 g

Refreshing Cucumber Lime

Ingredients:

- 1 medium cucumber

- 2 medium limes (peeled)

- 1 handful of mint leaves

Procedure:

1. Slice the cucumber and limes into chunks.

2. Wash the mint leaves.

3. Add all the ingredients to a juicer and extract the juice.

4. Stir the juice gently and serve chilled.

Calories: 80

Sugar: 10 g

Green Goddess

Ingredients:

- 2 cups spinach

- 1 medium cucumber

- 2 medium green apples

- 1-inch piece of ginger

Procedure:

1. Wash the spinach leaves thoroughly and remove any tough stems.

2. Slice the cucumber and green apples into chunks.

3. Peel and chop the ginger.

4. Add all the ingredients to a juicer and extract the juice.

5. Stir the juice gently and serve chilled.

Calories: 140

Sugar: 20 g

Pineapple Ginger Twist

Ingredients:

- 2 cups pineapple chunks

- 1 medium cucumber

- 1-inch piece of ginger

Procedure:

1. Slice the pineapple and cucumber into chunks.

2. Peel and chop the ginger.

3. Add all the ingredients to a juicer and extract the juice.

4. Stir the juice gently and serve chilled.

Calories: 130

Sugar: 15 g

Apple Carrot Glow

Ingredients:

- 2 medium apples

- 2 medium carrots

- 1 medium orange (peeled)

Procedure:

1. Slice the apples, carrots, and orange into chunks.

2. Add all the ingredients to a juicer and extract the juice.

3. Stir the juice gently and serve chilled.

Calories: 140

Sugar: 25 g

Green Detox Cleanse

Ingredients:

- 2 cups spinach
- 1 green apple
- 1/2 cucumber
- 1/2 lemon (peeled)
- 1 inch piece of ginger

Procedure:

1. Wash the spinach leaves thoroughly and remove any tough stems.
2. Slice the green apple and cucumber into chunks.
3. Peel the lemon.
4. Peel and chop the ginger.
5. Add all the ingredients to a juicer and extract the juice.
6. Stir the juice gently and serve chilled.

Calories: 90

Sugar: 10 g

Berry Blast Slimmer

Ingredients:

- 1 cup strawberries
- 1 cup blueberries
- 1 cup raspberries
- 1/2 cup unsweetened almond milk

Procedure:

1. Wash the berries.
2. Add the berries and almond milk to a blender and blend until smooth.
3. Pour the mixture into a glass and serve chilled.

Calories: 120

Sugar: 12 g

Cucumber Lime Refresher

Ingredients:

- 1/2 cucumber
- 1/2 cup mint leaves
- 1 lime (peeled)

Procedure:

1. Slice the cucumber.

2. Wash the mint leaves.

3. Peel the lime.

4. Add all the ingredients to a blender and blend until smooth.

5. Pour the mixture into a glass and serve chilled.

Calories: 60

Sugar: 8 g

Carrot Ginger Zing

Ingredients:

- 4 medium carrots
- 1 inch piece of ginger
- 1/2 lemon (peeled)

Procedure:

1. Wash and chop the carrots into chunks.

2. Peel and chop the ginger.

3. Peel the lemon.

4. Add all the ingredients to a juicer and extract the juice.

5. Stir the juice gently and serve chilled.

Calories: 90

Sugar: 10 g

Watermelon Mint Splash

Ingredients:

- 2 cups watermelon chunks
- 1/2 cup mint leaves
- 1/2 lime (peeled)

Procedure:

1. Slice the watermelon into chunks.
2. Wash the mint leaves.
3. Peel the lime.
4. Add all the ingredients to a blender and blend until smooth.
5. Pour the mixture into a glass and serve chilled.

Calories: 80

Sugar: 10 g

Pineapple Kale Kick

Ingredients:

- 2 cups pineapple chunks
- 2 cups kale
- 1/2 cucumber
- 1/2 lemon (peeled)

Procedure:

1. Slice the pineapple into chunks.

2. Wash the kale leaves thoroughly and remove any tough stems.

3. Slice the cucumber.

4. Peel the lemon.

5. Add all the ingredients to a juicer and extract the juice.

6. Stir the juice gently and serve chilled.

Calories: 110

Sugar: 12 g

Grapefruit Detox Delight

Ingredients:

- 1 grapefruit (peeled)

- 1 orange (peeled)

- 1/2 lemon (peeled)

Procedure:

1. Peel the grapefruit, orange, and lemon.

2. Add all the ingredients to a juicer and extract the juice.

3. Stir the juice gently and serve chilled.

Calories: 80

Sugar: 10 g

Beet Berry Blast

Ingredients:

- 1 medium beetroot (peeled)
- 1 cup mixed berries (strawberries, blueberries, raspberries)
- 1/2 lemon (peeled)

Procedure:

1. Wash and chop the beetroot into chunks.
2. Wash the berries.
3. Peel the lemon.
4. Add all the ingredients to a juicer and extract the juice.
5. Stir the juice gently and serve chilled.

Calories: 110

Sugar: 12 g

Apple Celery Slimmer

Ingredients:

- 2 medium apples
- 2 stalks of celery
- 1/2 lemon (peeled)

Procedure:

1. Slice the apples and celery.

2. Peel the lemon.

3. Add all the ingredients to a juicer and extract the juice.

4. Stir the juice gently and serve chilled.

Calories: 100

Sugar: 12 g

Pineapple Spinach Slim Down

Ingredients:

- 2 cups pineapple chunks

- 2 cups spinach

- 1/2 cucumber

- 1/2 lime (peeled)

Procedure:

1. Slice the pineapple into chunks.

2. Wash the spinach leaves thoroughly and remove any tough stems.

3. Slice the cucumber.

4. Peel the lime.

5. Add all the ingredients to a juicer and extract the juice.

6. Stir the juice gently and serve chilled.

Calories: 120

Sugar: 14 g

10 Juice Recipes for Detox:

Green Detox Elixir With Spinach

Ingredients:

- 2 cups spinach
- 1 green apple
- 1/2 cucumber
- 1/2 lemon (peeled)
- 1 inch piece of ginger

Procedure:

1. Wash the spinach leaves thoroughly and remove any tough stems.
2. Slice the green apple and cucumber into chunks.
3. Peel the lemon.
4. Peel and chop the ginger.
5. Add all the ingredients to a juicer and extract the juice.
6. Stir the juice gently and serve chilled.

Calories: 90

Sugar: 10 g

Beet Detox Power

Ingredients:

- 2 medium beetroots (peeled)

- 2 medium carrots

- 1/2 lemon (peeled)

Procedure:

1. Wash and chop the beetroots and carrots into chunks.

2. Peel the lemon.

3. Add all the ingredients to a juicer and extract the juice.

4. Stir the juice gently and serve chilled.

Calories: 110

Sugar: 12 g

Citrus Detox Zing

Ingredients:

- 2 oranges (peeled)

- 1 grapefruit (peeled)

- 1/2 lemon (peeled)

Procedure:

1. Peel the oranges, grapefruit, and lemon.

2. Add all the ingredients to a juicer and extract the juice.

3. Stir the juice gently and serve chilled.

Calories: 90

Sugar: 10 g

Pineapple Ginger Cleanse

Ingredients:

- 2 cups pineapple chunks
- 1/2 inch piece of ginger
- 1/2 lemon (peeled)

Procedure:

1. Slice the pineapple into chunks.
2. Peel and chop the ginger.
3. Peel the lemon.
4. Add all the ingredients to a juicer and extract the juice.
5. Stir the juice gently and serve chilled.

Calories: 100

Sugar: 12 g

Ginger Turmeric Cleanse

Ingredients:

- 1/2 inch piece of ginger

- 1/2 inch piece of turmeric root (or 1/2 teaspoon turmeric powder)

- 1 orange (peeled)

- 1/2 lemon (peeled)

- 1 tablespoon honey (optional)

Procedure:

1. Peel and chop the ginger and turmeric root.

2. Peel the orange and lemon.

3. Add all the ingredients to a juicer and extract the juice.

4. Stir the juice gently and serve chilled.

Calories: 80

Sugar: 10 g

Papaya Pineapple Detox

Ingredients:

- 2 cups papaya chunks

- 2 cups pineapple chunks

- 1/2 lime (peeled)

Procedure:

1. Slice the papaya and pineapple into chunks.

2. Peel the lime.

3. Add all the ingredients to a blender and blend until smooth.

4. Pour the mixture into a glass and serve chilled.

Calories: 140

Sugar: 16 g

Watermelon Cucumber Cooler

Ingredients:

- 2 cups watermelon chunks
- 1/2 cucumber
- 1/2 lime (peeled)
- 1 tablespoon fresh basil leaves

Procedure:

1. Slice the watermelon into chunks.
2. Slice the cucumber.
3. Peel the lime.
4. Wash the basil leaves.
5. Add all the ingredients to a blender and blend until smooth.
6. Pour the mixture into a glass and serve chilled.

Calories: 80

Sugar: 10 g

Carrot Orange Detoxifier

Ingredients:

- 4 medium carrots
- 2 oranges (peeled)
- 1/2 lemon (peeled)

Procedure:

1. Wash and chop the carrots into chunks.
2. Peel the oranges and lemon.
3. Add all the ingredients to a juicer and extract the juice.
4. Stir the juice gently and serve chilled.

Calories: 100

Sugar: 12 g

Minty Berry Cleanse

Ingredients:

- 1 cup strawberries
- 1 cup blueberries
- 1 cup raspberries
- 1/2 cup fresh mint leaves
- 1/2 lemon (peeled)

Procedure:

1. Wash the berries.

2. Wash the

mint leaves.

3. Peel the lemon.

4. Add all the ingredients to a blender and blend until smooth.

5. Pour the mixture into a glass and serve chilled.

Calories: 120

Sugar: 14 g

Revitalizing Green Cleanse

Ingredients:

- 2 cups spinach
- 1 cucumber
- 2 stalks celery
- 1 green apple
- 1/2 lemon (peeled)
- 1-inch piece of ginger

Procedure:

1. Wash the spinach thoroughly and remove any tough stems.
2. Slice the cucumber, celery, and green apple into chunks.
3. Peel the lemon.
4. Peel and chop the ginger.
5. Add all the ingredients to a juicer and extract the juice.
6. Stir the juice gently and serve chilled.

Calories: 130

Sugar: 15 g

Citrus Detox Blast

Ingredients:

- 2 oranges

- 1 grapefruit

- 1 lemon (peeled)

- 1 lime (peeled)

- 1/2 inch turmeric root (optional)

Procedure:

1. Peel the oranges, grapefruit, lemon, and lime.

2. If using turmeric root, peel and chop it into small pieces.

3. Add all the ingredients to a juicer and extract the juice.

4. Stir the juice gently and serve chilled.

Calories: 100

Sugar: 15 g

Beetroot Power Cleanse

Ingredients:

- 2 medium beetroots (peeled)

- 4 medium carrots

- 1 apple

- 1/2 lemon (peeled)

Procedure:

1. Wash and chop the beetroots, carrots, and apple into chunks.

2. Peel the lemon.

3. Add all the ingredients to a juicer and extract the juice.

4. Stir the juice gently and serve chilled.

Calories: 150

Sugar: 20 g

Berry Antioxidant Detox Blend

Ingredients:

- 1 cup strawberries
- 1 cup blueberries
- 1 cup raspberries
- 1 medium cucumber
- 1/2 lemon (peeled)

Procedure:

1. Wash the berries and cucumber.

2. Slice the cucumber into chunks.

3. Peel the lemon.

4. Add all the ingredients to a juicer and extract the juice.

5. Stir the juice gently and serve chilled.

Calories: 120

Sugar: 15 g

Green Ginger Detox Elixir

Ingredients:

- 2 cups kale
- 1 cucumber
- 1 green apple
- 1/2 lemon (peeled)
- 1-inch piece of ginger

Procedure:

1. Wash the kale leaves thoroughly and remove any tough stems.
2. Slice the cucumber and green apple into chunks.
3. Peel the lemon.
4. Peel and chop the ginger.
5. Add all the ingredients to a juicer and extract the juice.
6. Stir the juice gently and serve chilled.

Calories: 130

Sugar: 15 g

Pineapple Mint Detox Refresher

Ingredients:

- 2 cups pineapple chunks
- 1 medium cucumber
- 1/2 lime (peeled)
- 1 handful of fresh mint leaves

Procedure:

1. Slice the pineapple and cucumber into chunks.
2. Peel the lime.
3. Wash the mint leaves.
4. Add all the ingredients to a juicer and extract the juice.
5. Stir the juice gently and serve chilled.

Calories: 120

Sugar: 20 g

Carrot Turmeric Cleansing Elixir

Ingredients:

- 4 medium carrots
- 1 medium orange (peeled)
- 1/2 lemon (peeled)
- 1/2 inch turmeric root (optional)

Procedure:

1. Wash and chop the carrots into chunks.

2. Peel the orange and lemon.

3. If using turmeric root, peel and chop it into small pieces.

4. Add all the ingredients to a juicer and extract the juice.

5. Stir the juice gently and serve chilled.

Calories: 100

Sugar: 15 g

Refreshing Green Detox Delight

Ingredients:

- 2 cups spinach
- 1 medium cucumber
- 2 stalks celery
- 1/2 green apple
- 1/2 lemon (peeled)

Procedure:

1. Wash the spinach thoroughly and remove any tough stems.

2. Slice the cucumber, celery, and green apple into chunks.

3. Peel the lemon.

4. Add all the ingredients to a juicer and extract the juice.

5. Stir the juice gently and serve chilled.

Calories: 90

Sugar: 10 g

Cabbage Cleansing Elixir

Ingredients:

- 2 cups cabbage (any variety)
- 1 medium green apple
- 1/2 lemon (peeled)
- 1/2 inch ginger root (optional)

Procedure:

1. Slice the cabbage and green apple into chunks.
2. Peel the lemon.
3. If using ginger root, peel and chop it into small pieces.
4. Add all the ingredients to a juicer and extract the juice.
5. Stir the juice gently and serve chilled.

Calories: 80

Sugar: 15 g

Watermelon Mint Detox Splash

Ingredients:

- 2 cups watermelon chunks
- 1/2 cucumber
- 1/2 lime (peeled)
- 1 handful of fresh mint leaves

Procedure:

1. Slice the watermelon and cucumber into chunks.
2. Peel the lime.
3. Wash the mint leaves.
4. Add all the ingredients to a juicer and extract the juice.
5. Stir the juice gently and serve chilled.

Calories: 80

Sugar: 10 g

Vitamin C Power Boost

Ingredients:

- 2 oranges
- 1 grapefruit
- 1 lemon (peeled)
- 1-inch piece of ginger

Procedure:

1. Peel the oranges, grapefruit, and lemon.

2. Peel and chop the ginger.

3. Add all the ingredients to a juicer and extract the juice.

4. Stir the juice gently and serve chilled.

Calories: 100

Sugar: 15 g

Green Immunity Elixir

Title: "Leafy Green Vitality"

Ingredients:

- 2 cups spinach
- 1 cucumber
- 2 stalks celery
- 1 green apple
- 1/2 lemon (peeled)
- 1-inch piece of ginger

Procedure:

1. Wash the spinach leaves thoroughly and remove any tough stems.

2. Slice the cucumber, celery, and green apple into chunks.

3. Peel the lemon.

4. Peel and chop the ginger.

5. Add all the ingredients to a juicer and extract the juice.

6. Stir the juice gently and serve chilled.

Calories: 120

Sugar: 15 g

Antioxidant Berry Boost

Ingredients:

- 1 cup strawberries
- 1 cup blueberries
- 1 cup raspberries
- 1 medium orange (peeled)

Procedure:

1. Wash the berries.

2. Peel the orange.

3. Add all the ingredients to a juicer and extract the juice.

4. Stir the juice gently and serve chilled.

Calories: 150

Sugar: 20 g

Spicy Immune Kick

Ingredients:

- 1 medium orange (peeled)
- 1/2 lemon (peeled)
- 1-inch piece of ginger
- 1-inch piece of turmeric root (or 1/2 teaspoon turmeric powder)

Procedure:

1. Peel the orange and lemon.
2. Peel and chop the ginger and turmeric root.
3. Add all the ingredients to a juicer and extract the juice.
4. Stir the juice gently and serve chilled.

Calories: 80

Sugar: 10 g

Carrot Citrus Boost

Ingredients:

- 4 medium carrots
- 2 medium oranges (peeled)
- 1/2 lemon (peeled)

Procedure:

1. Wash and chop the carrots into chunks.

2. Peel the oranges and lemon.

3. Add all the ingredients to a juicer and extract the juice.

4. Stir the juice gently and serve chilled.

Calories: 100

Sugar: 15 g

Tropical Immunity Tonic

Ingredients:

- 2 cups pineapple chunks
- 1 medium orange (peeled)
- 1-inch piece of turmeric root (or 1/2 teaspoon turmeric powder)

Procedure:

1. Slice the pineapple into chunks.

2. Peel the orange.

3. Peel and chop the turmeric root.

4. Add all the ingredients to a juicer and extract the juice.

5. Stir the juice gently and serve chilled.

Calories: 130

Sugar: 20 g

Zesty Green Apple Boost

Ingredients:

- 2 green apples

- 1/2 lemon (peeled)

- 1-inch piece of ginger

Procedure:

1. Slice the green apples into chunks.

2. Peel the lemon.

3. Peel and chop the ginger.

4. Add all the ingredients to a juicer and extract the juice.

5. Stir the juice gently and serve chilled.

Calories: 120

Sugar: 15 g

Mango Carrot Immunity Blend

Ingredients:

- 1 medium mango (peeled and pitted)

- 2 medium carrots

- 1 medium orange (peeled)

Procedure:

1. Slice the mango and carrots into chunks.

2. Peel the orange.

3. Add all the ingredients to a juicer and extract the juice.

4. Stir the juice gently and serve chilled.

Calories: 140

Sugar: 25 g

Red Bell Pepper Vitality

Ingredients:

- 1 large red bell pepper
- 2 medium carrots
- 1 medium orange (peeled)

Procedure:

1. Slice the red bell pepper and carrots into chunks.

2. Peel the orange.

3. Add all the ingredients to a juicer and extract the juice.

4. Stir the juice gently and serve chilled.

Calories: 110

Sugar: 20 g

Refreshing Melon Cooler

Ingredients:

- 2 cups watermelon chunks
- 1/2 lime (peeled)

Procedure:

1. Slice the watermelon into chunks.
2. Peel the lime.
3. Add all the ingredients to a juicer and extract the juice.
4. Stir the juice gently and serve chilled.

Calories: 80

Sugar: 10 g

INCREASE ENERGY AND VITALITY

Supercharged Green Energy

Ingredients:

- 2 cups spinach
- 1 cucumber
- 2 stalks celery
- 1 green apple
- 1/2 lemon (peeled)
- 1-inch piece of ginger

Procedure:

1. Wash the spinach leaves thoroughly and remove any tough stems.
2. Slice the cucumber, celery, and green apple into chunks.
3. Peel the lemon.
4. Peel and chop the ginger.
5. Add all the ingredients to a juicer and extract the juice.
6. Stir the juice gently and serve chilled.

Calories: 120

Sugar: 15 g

Refreshing Citrus Burst

Ingredients:

- 2 oranges

- 1 grapefruit

- 1 lemon (peeled)

- 1 lime (peeled)

Procedure:

1. Peel the oranges, grapefruit, lemon, and lime.

2. Add all the ingredients to a juicer and extract the juice.

3. Stir the juice gently and serve chilled.

Calories: 100

Sugar: 15 g

Berry Power Boost

Ingredients:

- 1 cup strawberries

- 1 cup blueberries

- 1 cup raspberries

- 1 medium banana

- 1/2 cup almond milk (or any preferred plant-based milk)

Procedure:

1. Wash the berries.

2. Peel the banana.

3. Add all the ingredients to a blender and blend until smooth.

4. Pour the mixture into a glass and serve chilled.

Calories: 150

Sugar: 15 g

Tropical Energy Refresher

Ingredients:

- 2 cups pineapple chunks
- 1/2 lemon (peeled)
- 1-inch piece of ginger

Procedure:

1. Slice the pineapple into chunks.

2. Peel the lemon.

3. Peel and chop the ginger.

4. Add all the ingredients to a juicer and extract the juice.

5. Stir the juice gently and serve chilled.

Calories: 130

Sugar: 20 g

Zesty Green Revitalizer

Ingredients:

- 2 green apples
- 1/2 lemon (peeled)
- 1 handful of fresh mint leaves

Procedure:

1. Slice the green apples into chunks.
2. Peel the lemon.
3. Wash the mint leaves.
4. Add all the ingredients to a juicer and extract the juice.
5. Stir the juice gently and serve chilled.

Calories: 120

Sugar: 15 g

Carrot Ginger Power Boost

Ingredients:

- 4 medium carrots
- 1 orange (peeled)
- 1/2 lemon (peeled)

- 1-inch piece of ginger

Procedure:

1. Wash and chop the carrots into chunks.
2. Peel the orange and lemon.
3. Peel and chop the ginger.
4. Add all the ingredients to a juicer and extract the juice.
5. Stir the juice gently and serve chilled.

Calories: 100

Sugar: 15 g

Tropical Coconut Energizer

Ingredients:

- 1 medium mango (peeled and pitted)
- 1/2 cup coconut water
- 1/2 lime (peeled)

Procedure:

1. Slice the mango into chunks.
2. Add the mango chunks, coconut water, and peeled lime to a blender.
3. Blend until smooth.
4. Pour the mixture into a glass and serve chilled.

Calories: 150

Sugar: 25 g

Refreshing Watermelon Revive

Ingredients:

- 2 cups watermelon chunks

- 1/2 lime (peeled)

- 1 handful of fresh mint leaves

Procedure:

1. Slice the watermelon into chunks.

2. Peel the lime.

3. Wash the mint leaves.

4. Add all the ingredients to a juicer and extract the juice.

5. Stir the juice gently and serve chilled.

Calories: 80

Sugar: 10 g

Pineapple Kale Power Punch

Ingredients:

- 2 cups pineapple chunks

- 2 cups kale

- 1/2 lemon (peeled)

- 1 medium apple

Procedure:

1. Slice the pineapple into chunks.

2. Wash the kale leaves thoroughly and remove any tough stems.

3. Peel the lemon.

4. Slice the apple into chunks.

5. Add all the ingredients to a juicer and extract the juice.

6. Stir the juice gently and serve chilled.

Calories: 140

Sugar: 20 g

Beetroot Citrus Energizer

Ingredients:

- 2 medium beetroots (peeled)

- 2 medium oranges (peeled)

- 1/2 lemon (peeled)

Procedure:

1. Wash and chop the beetroots into chunks.

2. Peel the oranges and lemon.

3. Add all the ingredients to a juicer and extract the juice.

4. Stir the juice gently and serve chilled.

Calories: 140

Sugar: 20 g

10 Juice Recipes for Energy and Vitality:

Energizing Green Power

Ingredients:

- 2 cups spinach
- 1 green apple
- 1 cucumber
- 1/2 lemon (peeled)
- 1-inch piece of ginger

Procedure:

1. Wash the spinach leaves thoroughly and remove any tough stems.

2. Slice the green apple and cucumber into chunks.

3. Peel the lemon.

4. Peel and chop the ginger.

5. Add all the ingredients to a juicer and extract the juice.

6. Stir the juice gently and serve chilled.

Calories: 120

Sugar: 15 g

Tropical Energy Boost

Ingredients:

- 1 cup pineapple chunks
- 1 ripe banana
- 1 orange (peeled)
- 1/2 lime (peeled)

Procedure:

1. Slice the pineapple.
2. Peel the banana, orange, and lime.
3. Add all the ingredients to a blender and blend until smooth.
4. Pour the mixture into a glass and serve chilled.

Calories: 150

Sugar: 20 g

Refreshing Beet Berry Burst

Ingredients:

- 1 medium beetroot (peeled)
- 1 cup mixed berries (strawberries, blueberries, raspberries)
- 1/2 lemon (peeled)

Procedure:

1. Wash and chop the beetroot into chunks.
2. Wash the berries.
3. Peel the lemon.
4. Add all the ingredients to a juicer and extract the juice.
5. Stir the juice gently and serve chilled.

Calories: 130

Sugar: 15 g

Citrus Carrot Recharge

Ingredients:

- 4 medium carrots
- 2 oranges (peeled)
- 1/2 lemon (peeled)

Procedure:

1. Wash and chop the carrots into chunks.

2. Peel the oranges and lemon.

3. Add all the ingredients to a juicer and extract the juice.

4. Stir the juice gently and serve chilled.

Calories: 120

Sugar: 15 g

Green Power Punch

Ingredients:

- 2 cups kale
- 1 green apple
- 1 cucumber
- 1/2 lemon (peeled)
- 1-inch piece of ginger

Procedure:

1. Wash the kale leaves thoroughly and remove any tough stems.

2. Slice the green apple and cucumber into chunks.

3. Peel the lemon.

4. Peel and chop the ginger.

5. Add all the ingredients to a juicer and extract the juice.

6. Stir the juice gently and serve chilled.

Calories: 110

Sugar: 15 g

Minty Pineapple Boost

Ingredients:

- 2 cups pineapple chunks
- 1 handful of fresh mint leaves
- 1/2 lime (peeled)

Procedure:

1. Slice the pineapple into chunks.
2. Wash the mint leaves.
3. Peel the lime.
4. Add all the ingredients to a juicer and extract the juice.
5. Stir the juice gently and serve chilled.

Calories: 140

Sugar: 20 g

Berry Blast Energizer

Ingredients:

- 1 cup strawberries
- 1 cup blueberries
- 1 cup raspberries
- 1/2 banana

Procedure:

1. Wash the berries.
2. Peel the banana.
3. Add all the ingredients to a blender and blend until smooth.
4. Pour the mixture into a glass and serve chilled.

Calories: 130

Sugar: 15 g

Leafy Green Digestive Cleanser

Ingredients:

- 2 cups spinach
- 1 cucumber
- 2 stalks celery
- 1/2 green apple
- 1/2 lemon (peeled)
- 1-inch piece of ginger

Procedure:

1. Wash the spinach leaves thoroughly and remove any tough stems.
2. Slice the cucumber, celery, and green apple into chunks.
3. Peel the lemon.
4. Peel and chop the ginger.
5. Add all the ingredients to a juicer nd extract the juice.
6. Stir the juice gently and serve chilled.

Calories: 120

Sugar: 15 g

Tropical Digestive Soother

Ingredients:

- 2 cups pineapple chunks
- 1 cup papaya chunks
- 1/2 lime (peeled)

Procedure:

1. Slice the pineapple and papaya into chunks.
2. Peel the lime.
3. Add all the ingredients to a juicer and extract the juice.
4. Stir the juice gently and serve chilled.

Calories: 140

Sugar: 20 g

Carrot Ginger Digestive Tonic

Ingredients:

- 4 medium carrots
- 1 orange (peeled)
- 1/2 lemon (peeled)
- 1-inch piece of ginger

Procedure:

1. Wash and chop the carrots into chunks.

2. Peel the orange and lemon.

3. Peel and chop the ginger.

4. Add all the ingredients to a juicer and extract the juice.

5. Stir the juice gently and serve chilled.

Calories: 100

Sugar: 15 g

Cooling Digestive Refresher

Ingredients:

- 1 medium cucumber
- 2 limes (peeled)
- 1 handful of fresh mint leaves

Procedure:

1. Slice the cucumber and limes into chunks.

2. Wash the mint leaves.

3. Add all the ingredients to a juicer and extract the juice.

4. Stir the juice gently and serve chilled.

Calories: 80

Sugar: 10 g

Apple Celery Digestive Cleanse

Ingredients:

- 2 green apples

- 4 stalks celery

- 1/2 lemon (peeled)

Procedure:

1. Slice the green apples into chunks.

2. Chop the celery stalks.

3. Peel the lemon.

4. Add all the ingredients to a juicer and extract the juice.

5. Stir the juice gently and serve chilled.

Calories: 120

Sugar: 15 g

Ginger Turmeric Digestive Tonic

Ingredients:

- 1/2 lemon (peeled)

- 1/2 inch piece of ginger

- 1/2 inch piece of turmeric root (or 1/2 teaspoon turmeric powder)

Procedure:

1. Peel the lemon.

2. Peel and chop the ginger and turmeric root.

3. Add all the ingredients to a juicer and extract the juice.

4. Stir the juice gently and serve chilled.

Calories: 60

Sugar: 5 g

Papaya Mint Digestive Refresher

Ingredients:

- 2 cups papaya chunks
- 1/2 lime (peeled)
- 1 handful of fresh mint leaves

Procedure:

1. Slice the papaya into chunks.

2. Peel the lime.

3. Wash the mint leaves.

4. Add all the ingredients to a juicer and extract the juice.

5. Stir the juice gently and serve chilled.

Calories: 120

Sugar: 20 g

Pineapple Ginger Digestive Aid

Ingredients:

- 2 cups pineapple chunks
- 1/2 lemon (peeled)
- 1-inch piece of ginger

Procedure:

1. Slice the pineapple into chunks.
2. Peel the lemon.
3. Peel and chop the ginger.
4. Add all the ingredients to a juicer and extract the juice.
5. Stir the juice gently and serve chilled.

Calories: 130

Sugar: 20 g

Beetroot Carrot Digestive Booster

Ingredients:

- 2 medium beetroots (peeled)
- 4 medium carrots

- 1/2 lemon (peeled)

Procedure:

1. Wash and chop the beetroots and carrots into chunks.

2. Peel the lemon.

3. Add all the ingredients to a juicer and extract the juice.

4. Stir the juice gently and serve chilled.

Calories: 140

Sugar: 20 g

Green Apple Aloe Digestive Soother

Ingredients:

- 2 green apples

- 1/2 lemon (peeled)

- 1/2

cup aloe vera juice

Procedure:

1. Slice the green apples into chunks.

2. Peel the lemon.

3. Add all the ingredients to a juicer and extract the juice.

4. Stir the juice gently and serve chilled.

Calories: 140

Sugar: 20 g

Ginger Lemon Detox

Ingredients:

- 1 inch piece of ginger
- 1/2 lemon (peeled)
- 1 cucumber
- 1 cup spinach

Procedure:

1. Peel and chop the ginger.
2. Peel the lemon.
3. Slice the cucumber.
4. Wash the spinach leaves thoroughly and remove any tough stems.
5. Add all the ingredients to a juicer and extract the juice.
6. Stir the juice gently and serve chilled.

Calories: 70

Sugar: 10 g

Pineapple Mint Cooler

Ingredients:

- 2 cups pineapple chunks
- 1 handful of fresh mint leaves
- 1/2 cucumber

Procedure:

1. Slice the pineapple into chunks.
2. Wash the mint leaves.
3. Slice the cucumber.
4. Add all the ingredients to a juicer and extract the juice.
5. Stir the juice gently and serve chilled.

Calories: 100

Sugar: 15 g

Green Detox Delight

Ingredients:

- 2 cups kale
- 1 green apple
- 1/2 cucumber
- 1/2 lemon (peeled)
- 1/2 inch piece of ginger

Procedure:

1. Wash the kale leaves thoroughly and remove any tough stems.

2. Slice the green apple and cucumber into chunks.

3. Peel the lemon.

4. Peel and chop the ginger.

5. Add all the ingredients to a juicer and extract the juice.

6. Stir the juice gently and serve chilled.

Calories: 90

Sugar: 10 g

Beetroot Carrot Cleanse

Ingredients:

- 1 medium beetroot (peeled)

- 4 medium carrots

- 1/2 inch piece of ginger

Procedure:

1. Wash and chop the beetroot into chunks.

2. Wash and chop the carrots into chunks.

3. Peel and chop the ginger.

4. Add all the ingredients to a juicer and extract the juice.

5. Stir the juice gently and serve chilled.

Calories: 120

Sugar: 15 g

Papaya Digestive Soother

Ingredients:

- 2 cups papaya chunks
- 1/2 lime (peeled)
- 1 tablespoon honey (optional)

Procedure:

1. Slice the papaya into chunks.
2. Peel the lime.
3. Add all the ingredients to a blender and blend until smooth.
4. Pour the mixture into a glass and serve chilled.

Calories: 120

Sugar: 15 g

Cucumber Celery Refresher

Ingredients:

- 1/2 cucumber
- 2 stalks of celery
- 1/2 lemon (peeled)

- 1 handful of fresh parsley

Procedure:

1. Slice the cucumber and celery.

2. Peel the lemon.

3. Wash the parsley.

4. Add all the ingredients to a juicer and extract the juice.

5. Stir the juice gently and serve chilled.

Calories: 50

Sugar: 5 g

Mango Ginger Cleanse

Ingredients:

- 1 medium mango (peeled and pitted)

- 1 inch piece of ginger

- 1/2 lemon (peeled)

Procedure:

1. Slice the mango into chunks.

2. Peel and chop the ginger.

3. Peel the lemon.

4. Add all the ingredients to a juicer and extract the juice.

5. Stir the juice gently and serve chilled.

Calories: 120

Sugar: 15 g

Carrot Apple Refresher

Ingredients:

- 4 medium carrots
- 2 medium apples
- 1/2 inch piece of ginger

Procedure:

1. Wash and chop the carrots into chunks.
2. Slice the apples into chunks.
3. Peel and chop the ginger.
4. Add all the ingredients to a juicer and extract the juice.
5. Stir the juice gently and serve chilled.

Calories: 120

Sugar: 15 g

Watermelon Basil Cleanse

Ingredients:

- 2 cups watermelon chunks

- 1 handful of fresh basil leaves

- 1/2 lime (peeled)

Procedure:

1. Slice the watermelon into chunks.

2. Wash the basil leaves.

3. Peel the lime.

4. Add all the ingredients to a juicer and extract the juice.

5. Stir the juice gently and serve chilled.

Calories: 70

Sugar: 10 g

Pear Spinach Cleanse

Ingredients:

- 2 medium pears

- 2 cups spinach

- 1/2 lemon (peeled)

Procedure:

1. Slice the pears into chunks.
2. Wash the spinach leaves thoroughly and remove any tough stems.
3. Peel the lemon.
4. Add all the ingredients to a juicer and extract the juice.
5. Stir the juice gently and serve chilled.

Calories: 110

Sugar: 15 g

HEART HEALTH

Berry Heart Booster With Orange

Ingredients:

- 1 cup strawberries
- 1 cup blueberries
- 1 cup raspberries
- 1 medium orange (peeled)

Procedure:

1. Wash the berries.
2. Peel the orange.
3. Add all the ingredients to a juicer and extract the juice.
4. Stir the juice gently and serve chilled.

Calories: 150

Sugar: 20 g

Beetroot Apple Elixir

Ingredients:

- 2 medium beetroots (peeled)
- 2 green apples

- 1/2 lemon (peeled)

Procedure:

1. Wash and chop the beetroots into chunks.

2. Slice the green apples into chunks.

3. Peel the lemon.

4. Add all the ingredients to a juicer and extract the juice.

5. Stir the juice gently and serve chilled.

Calories: 140

Sugar: 20 g

Citrus Kale Cleanse

Ingredients:

- 2 cups kale

- 2 medium oranges (peeled)

- 1/2 lemon (peeled)

Procedure:

1. Wash the kale leaves thoroughly and remove any tough stems.

2. Peel the oranges and lemon.

3. Add all the ingredients to a juicer and extract the juice.

4. Stir the juice gently and serve chilled.

Calories: 100

Sugar: 15 g

Pomegranate Beet Blend

Ingredients:

- 1 medium beetroot (peeled)

- 1 cup pomegranate seeds

- 1/2 lemon (peeled)

Procedure:

1. Wash and chop the beetroot into chunks.

2. Add the pomegranate seeds to a blender.

3. Peel the lemon.

4. Add all the ingredients to a juicer and extract the juice.

5. Stir the juice gently and serve chilled.

Calories: 120

Sugar: 15 g

Green Apple Spinach Delight

Ingredients:

- 2 green apples

- 2 cups spinach

- 1/2 lemon (peeled)

Procedure:

1. Slice the green apples into chunks.

2. Wash the spinach leaves thoroughly and remove any tough stems.

3. Peel the lemon.

4. Add all the ingredients to a juicer and extract the juice.

5. Stir the juice gently and serve chilled.

Calories: 120

Sugar: 15 g

Carrot Ginger Splash

Ingredients:

- 4 medium carrots

- 1 orange (peeled)

- 1/2 lemon (peeled)

- 1-inch piece of ginger

Procedure:

1. Wash and chop the carrots into chunks.

2. Peel the orange and lemon.

3. Peel and chop the ginger.

4. Add all the ingredients to a juicer and extract the juice.

5. Stir the juice gently and serve chilled.

Calories: 100

Sugar: 15 g

Turmeric Pineapple Punch

Ingredients:

- 2 cups pineapple chunks

- 1/2 lemon (peeled)

- 1-inch piece of turmeric root (or 1/2 teaspoon turmeric powder)

Procedure:

1. Slice the pineapple into chunks.

2. Peel the lemon.

3. Peel and chop the turmeric root.

4. Add all the ingredients to a juicer and extract the juice.

5. Stir the juice gently and serve chilled.

Calories: 130

Sugar: 20 g

Spinach Avocado Heart Boost

Ingredients:

- 2 cups spinach
- 1/2 avocado
- 1 medium green apple
- 1/2 lemon (peeled)

Procedure:

1. Wash the spinach leaves thoroughly and remove any tough stems.
2. Scoop out the flesh of the avocado.
3. Slice the green apple into chunks.
4. Peel the lemon.
5. Add all the ingredients to a juicer and extract the juice.
6. Stir the juice gently and serve chilled.

Calories: 150

Sugar: 15 g

Celery Cucumber Cooler

Ingredients:

- 2 stalks celery
- 1/2 cucumber
- 1/2 lemon (peeled)

Procedure:

1. Chop the celery stalks.

2. Slice the cucumber into chunks.

3. Peel the lemon.

4. Add all the ingredients to a juicer and extract the juice.

5. Stir the juice gently and serve chilled.

Calories: 40

Sugar: 5 g

Apple Beet Detox

Ingredients:

- 2 green apples

- 1 medium beetroot (peeled)

- 1/2 lemon (peeled)

Procedure:

1. Slice the green apples into chunks.

2. Chop the beetroot into chunks.

3. Peel the lemon.

4. Add all the ingredients to a juicer and extract the juice.

5. Stir the juice gently and serve chilled.

Calories: 140

Sugar: 20 g

Ginger Orange Zing

Ingredients:

- 2 medium oranges (peeled)

- 1/2 lemon (peeled)

- 1-inch piece of ginger

Procedure:

1. Peel the oranges and lemon.

2. Peel and chop the ginger.

3. Add all the ingredients to a juicer and extract the juice.

4. Stir the juice gently and serve chilled.

Calories: 90

Sugar: 10 g

Kiwi Berry Delight

Ingredients:

- 2 kiwis (peeled)

- 1 cup strawberries

- 1 cup blueberries

Procedure:

1. Slice the kiwis.

2. Wash the strawberries and blueberries.

3. Add all the ingredients to a blender and blend until smooth.

4. Pour the mixture into a glass and serve chilled.

Calories: 130

Sugar: 20 g

Cucumber Mint Refresher

Ingredients:

- 1/2 cucumber
- 1/2 lime (peeled)
- 1 handful of fresh mint leaves

Procedure:

1. Slice the cucumber.

2. Peel the lime.

3. Wash the mint leaves.

4. Add all the ingredients to a juicer and extract the juice.

5. Stir the juice gently and serve chilled.

Calories: 40

Sugar: 5 g

Spinach Grapefruit Twist

Ingredients:

- 2 cups spinach
- 1 grapefruit (peeled)
- 1/2 lemon (peeled)

Procedure:

1. Wash the spinach leaves thoroughly and remove any tough stems.
2. Peel the grapefruit and lemon.
3. Add all the ingredients to a juicer and extract the juice.
4. Stir the juice gently and serve chilled.

Calories: 120

Sugar: 15 g

Mango Carrot Smoothie

Ingredients:

- 1 medium mango (peeled and pitted)
- 2 medium carrots
- 1/2 lemon (peeled)

Procedure:

1. Slice the mango into chunks.

2. Wash and chop the carrots into chunks.

3. Peel the lemon.

4. Add all the ingredients to a blender and blend until smooth.

5. Pour the mixture into a glass and serve chilled.

Calories: 150

Sugar: 20 g

Berry Heart Booster with Pomegranate

Ingredients:

- 1 cup strawberries
- 1 cup blueberries
- 1 cup raspberries
- 1/2 cup pomegranate seeds

Procedure:

1. Wash the berries and pomegranate seeds.

2. Add all the ingredients to a blender and blend until smooth.

3. Pour the mixture into a glass and serve chilled.

Calories: 120

Sugar: 15 g

Citrus Beet Power

Ingredients:

- 2 medium beetroots (peeled)

- 2 oranges (peeled)

- 1/2 lemon (peeled)

Procedure:

1. Wash and chop the beetroots into chunks.

2. Peel the oranges and lemon.

3. Add all the ingredients to a juicer and extract the juice.

4. Stir the juice gently and serve chilled.

Calories: 110

Sugar: 15 g

Apple Celery Refresher

Ingredients:

- 2 medium apples

- 2 stalks of celery

- 1/2 cucumber

- 1/2 lemon (peeled)

Procedure:

1. Slice the apples, celery, and cucumber.

2. Peel the lemon.

3. Add all the ingredients to a juicer and extract the juice.

4. Stir the juice gently and serve chilled.

Calories: 100

Sugar: 12 g

Spinach Tomato Elixir

Ingredients:

- 2 cups spinach
- 2 medium tomatoes
- 1/2 cucumber
- 1/2 lemon (peeled)

Procedure:

1. Wash the spinach leaves thoroughly and remove any tough stems.

2. Chop the tomatoes and cucumber.

3. Peel the lemon.

4. Add all the ingredients to a juicer and extract the juice.

5. Stir the juice gently and serve chilled.

Calories: 90

Sugar: 10 g

Grapefruit Ginger Zing

Ingredients:

- 1 grapefruit (peeled)
- 1/2 inch piece of ginger
- 1/2 lemon (peeled)

Procedure:

1. Peel the grapefruit and lemon.
2. Peel and chop the ginger.
3. Add all the ingredients to a juicer and extract the juice.
4. Stir the juice gently and serve chilled.

Calories: 70

Sugar: 8 g

Carrot Orange Antioxidant

Ingredients:

- 4 medium carrots
- 2 oranges (peeled)
- 1/2 lemon (peeled)

Procedure:

1. Wash and chop the carrots into chunks.

2. Peel the oranges and lemon.

3. Add all the ingredients to a juicer and extract the juice.

4. Stir the juice gently and serve chilled.

Calories: 120

Sugar: 15 g

Turmeric Pineapple Twist

Ingredients:

- 2 cups pineapple chunks
- 1/2 inch piece of turmeric root (or 1/2 teaspoon turmeric powder)
- 1/2 lemon (peeled)

Procedure:

1. Slice the pineapple into chunks.

2. Peel and chop the turmeric root.

3. Peel the lemon.

4. Add all the ingredients to a juicer and extract the juice.

5. Stir the juice gently and serve chilled.

Calories: 110

Sugar: 15 g

Papaya Mango Delight

Ingredients:

- 2 cups papaya chunks
- 1 medium mango (peeled and pitted)
- 1/2 lime (peeled)

Procedure:

1. Slice the papaya and mango into chunks.
2. Peel the lime.
3. Add all the ingredients to a blender and blend until smooth.
4. Pour the mixture into a glass and serve chilled.

Calories: 140

Sugar: 20 g

Cranberry Apple Fusion

Ingredients:

- 1 cup cranberries
- 2 medium apples
- 1/2 lemon (peeled)

Procedure:

1. Wash the cranberries.
2. Slice the apples into chunks.
3. Peel the lemon.
4. Add all the ingredients to a juicer and extract the juice.
5. Stir the juice gently and serve chilled.

Calories: 130

Sugar: 15 g

Watermelon Basil Crush

Ingredients:

- 2 cups watermelon chunks
- 1 handful of fresh basil leaves
- 1/2 lime (peeled)

Procedure:

1. Slice the watermelon into chunks.
2. Wash the basil leaves.
3. Peel the lime.
4. Add all the ingredients to a juicer and extract the juice.
5. Stir the juice gently and serve chilled.

Calories: 80

Sugar: 10 g

Enjoy these heart-healthy juice recipes! Remember to incorporate them as part of a balanced diet and consult with a healthcare professional if you have any specific health concerns.

Citrus Immune Kick

Ingredients:

- 2 oranges (peeled)
- 1 lemon (peeled)
- 1/2 inch piece of ginger
- 1 tablespoon honey (optional)

Procedure:

1. Peel the oranges and lemon.
2. Peel and chop the ginger.
3. Add all the ingredients to a juicer and extract the juice.
4. Stir the juice gently and serve chilled.

Calories: 120

Sugar: 15 g

Turmeric Carrot Booster

Ingredients:

- 4 medium carrots
- 1 inch piece of turmeric root (or 1/2 teaspoon turmeric powder)
- 1 orange (peeled)

Procedure:

1. Wash and chop the carrots into chunks.
2. Peel the orange.
3. Peel and chop the turmeric root.
4. Add all the ingredients to a juicer and extract the juice.
5. Stir the juice gently and serve chilled.

Calories: 110

Sugar: 15 g

Berry Immunity Blast

Ingredients:

- 1 cup strawberries
- 1 cup blueberries
- 1 cup raspberries
- 1/2 cup Greek yogurt
- 1 tablespoon honey (optional)

Procedure:

1. Wash the berries.

2. Add the berries, Greek yogurt, and honey (if desired) to a blender.

3. Blend until smooth.

4. Pour the mixture into a glass and serve chilled.

Calories: 150

Sugar: 15 g

Ginger Beet Elixir

Ingredients:

- 1 medium beetroot (peeled)

- 1 inch piece of ginger

- 1 medium apple

- 1/2 lemon (peeled)

Procedure:

1. Wash and chop the beetroot into chunks.

2. Peel and chop the ginger.

3. Slice the apple into chunks.

4. Peel the lemon.

5. Add all the ingredients to a juicer and extract the juice.

6. Stir the juice gently and serve chilled.

Calories: 120

Sugar: 15 g

Green Immunity Boost

Ingredients:

- 2 cups spinach
- 1 green apple
- 1 cucumber
- 1/2 lemon (peeled)
- 1 inch piece of ginger

Procedure:

1. Wash the spinach leaves thoroughly and remove any tough stems.
2. Slice the green apple and cucumber into chunks.
3. Peel the lemon.
4. Peel and chop the ginger.
5. Add all the ingredients to a juicer and extract the juice.
6. Stir the juice gently and serve chilled.

Calories: 110

Sugar: 15 g

Pineapple Ginger Immune Boost

Ingredients:

- 2 cups pineapple chunks
- 1/2 inch piece of ginger
- 1/2 lemon (peeled)
- 1 tablespoon honey (optional)

Procedure:

1. Slice the pineapple into chunks.
2. Peel and chop the ginger.
3. Peel the lemon.
4. Add all the ingredients to a juicer and extract the juice.
5. Stir the juice gently and serve chilled.

Calories: 130

Sugar: 20 g

Orange Carrot Sunshine

Ingredients:

- 4 medium carrots
- 2 oranges (peeled)
- 1/2 inch piece of turmeric root (or 1/2 teaspoon turmeric powder)

Procedure:

1. Wash and chop the carrots into chunks.

2. Peel the oranges.

3. Peel and chop the turmeric root.

4. Add all the ingredients to a juicer and extract the juice.

5. Stir the juice gently and serve chilled.

Calories: 120

Sugar: 15 g

Strawberry Kiwi Boost

Ingredients:

- 1 cup strawberries
- 2 kiwis (peeled)
- 1/2 lime (peeled)
- 1 tablespoon honey (optional)

Procedure:

1. Wash the strawberries.

2. Slice the kiwis.

3. Peel the lime.

4. Add all the ingredients to a blender and blend until smooth.

5. Pour the mixture into a glass and serve chilled.

Calories: 130

Sugar: 15 g

Cranberry Apple Defense

Ingredients:

- 1 cup cranberries
- 2 medium apples
- 1/2 lemon (peeled)
- 1 tablespoon honey (optional)

Procedure:

1. Wash the cranberries.
2. Slice the apples into chunks.
3. Peel the lemon.
4. Add all the ingredients to a juicer and extract the juice.
5. Stir the juice gently and serve chilled.

Calories: 140

Sugar: 20 g

Melon Mint Immune Refresher

Ingredients:

- 2 cups melon chunks (watermelon or cantaloupe)

- 1 handful of fresh mint leaves

- 1/2 lime (peeled)

Procedure:

1. Slice the melon into chunks.

2. Wash the mint leaves.

3. Peel the lime.

4. Add all the ingredients to a juicer and extract the juice.

5. Stir the juice gently and serve chilled.

Calories: 90

Sugar: 10 g

Ginger Carrot Sunrise

Ingredients:

- 3 medium carrots

- 1 orange (peeled)

- 1/2 inch piece of ginger

Procedure:

1. Wash and chop the carrots into chunks.

2. Peel the orange.

3. Peel and chop the ginger.

4. Add all the ingredients to a juicer and extract the juice.

5. Stir the juice gently and serve chilled.

Calories: 90

Sugar: 12 g

Turmeric Mango Sunrise

Ingredients:

- 1 medium mango (peeled and pitted)
- 1/2 cup coconut water
- 1/2 inch piece of turmeric root (or 1/2 teaspoon turmeric powder)

Procedure:

1. Slice the mango into chunks.
2. Peel and chop the turmeric root.
3. Add all the ingredients to a blender and blend until smooth.
4. Pour the mixture into a glass and serve chilled.

Calories: 140

Sugar: 20 g

Coconut Water Citrus Splash

Ingredients:

- 1 cup coconut water

- 1 orange (peeled)

- 1/2 grapefruit (peeled)

- 1/2 lime (peeled)

Procedure:

1. Peel the orange, grapefruit, and lime.

2. Add all the ingredients to a blender and blend until smooth.

3. Pour the mixture into a glass and serve chilled.

Calories: 90

Sugar: 10 g

Orange Strawberry Delight

Ingredients:

- 2 oranges (peeled)
- 1 cup strawberries

Procedure:

1. Peel the oranges.
2. Wash the strawberries.
3. Add all the ingredients to a juicer and extract the juice.
4. Stir the juice gently and serve chilled.

Calories: 100

Sugar: 15 g

Apple Carrot Crush

Ingredients:

- 2 medium apples
- 2 medium carrots

Procedure:

1. Slice the apples into chunks.

2. Wash and chop the carrots into chunks.

3. Add all the ingredients to a juicer and extract the juice.

4. Stir the juice gently and serve chilled.

Calories: 120

Sugar: 15 g

Tropical Paradise

Ingredients:

- 1 banana

- 1 cup pineapple chunks

- 1/2 cup coconut water (or regular water)

Procedure:

1. Peel the banana.

2. Slice the pineapple into chunks.

3. Add all the ingredients to a blender and blend until smooth.

4. Pour the mixture into a glass and serve chilled.

Calories: 150

Sugar: 20 g

Very Berry Blast

Ingredients:

- 1 cup strawberries

- 1 cup blueberries

- 1 cup raspberries

Procedure:

1. Wash the berries.

2. Add all the ingredients to a blender and blend until smooth.

3. Pour the mixture into a glass and serve chilled.

Calories: 120

Sugar: 15 g

Green Lemonade

Ingredients:

- 2 cups spinach

- 2 medium apples

- 1/2 lemon (peeled)

Procedure:

1. Wash the spinach leaves thoroughly and remove any tough stems.

2. Slice the apples into chunks.

3. Peel the lemon.

4. Add all the ingredients to a juicer and extract the juice.

5. Stir the juice gently and serve chilled.

Calories: 120

Sugar: 15 g

Cucumber Mint Cooler

Ingredients:

- 1/2 cucumber
- 1/2 lime (peeled)
- 1 handful of fresh mint leaves

Procedure:

1. Slice the cucumber.
2. Peel the lime.
3. Wash the mint leaves.
4. Add all the ingredients to a juicer and extract the juice.
5. Stir the juice gently and serve chilled.

Calories: 40

Sugar: 5 g

Watermelon Lime Quencher

Ingredients:

- 2 cups watermelon chunks

- 1/2 lime (peeled)

Procedure:

1. Slice the watermelon into chunks.

2. Peel the lime.

3. Add all the ingredients to a juicer and extract the juice.

4. Stir the juice gently and serve chilled.

Calories: 80

Sugar: 10 g

Pineapple Mango Punch

Ingredients:

- 1 cup pineapple chunks

- 1 medium mango (peeled and pitted)

Procedure:

1. Slice the pineapple and mango into chunks.

2. Add all the ingredients to a blender and blend until smooth.

3. Pour the mixture into a glass and serve chilled.

Calories: 140

Sugar: 20 g

Carrot Orange Sip

Ingredients:

- 3 medium carrots

- 2 oranges (peeled)

Procedure:

1. Wash and chop the carrots into chunks.

2. Peel the oranges.

3. Add all the ingredients to a juicer and extract the juice.

4. Stir the juice gently and serve chilled.

Calories: 120

Sugar: 15 g

Pineapple Kiwi Splash

Ingredients:

- 1 cup pineapple chunks

- 2 kiwis (peeled)

Procedure:

1. Slice the pineapple into chunks.

2. Slice the kiwis.

3. Add all the ingredients to a blender and blend until smooth.

4. Pour the mixture into a glass and serve chilled.

Calories: 120

Sugar: 15 g

CONCLUSION

As we get to the end of this juice recipe book, it's important to keep in mind that making great juices is only one aspect of a holistic approach to living a healthy life, and that a good diet, frequent physical activity, and stress management are all essential for our health and longevity.

The juices we've covered in this book are a great way to get a variety of nutrients that are good for you. These are great additions to a healthy diet, but don't forget to also eat enough of lean proteins, healthy fats, and complex carbohydrates! Exercising regularly not only aids in weight maintenance but also boosts mood and decreases stress.

Finally, we hope that this book has motivated you to improve your lifestyle by making healthier eating choices and include regular physical activity. Keep in mind that there isn't just one thing you can do to improve your chances of living a long and healthy life; rather, it's a combination of things. To everyone's health!

We appreciate you reading our book. We truly hope that you were entertained by our story and characters and that you appreciated it.

We respectfully ask you to take a few minutes to post an Amazon review if the book spoke to you and provided you with enjoyable moments. Your feedback is crucial to us and other readers who might be considering buying the book. Reviews help us develop as writers and give us a better understanding of what our readers find appealing.

It's easy to write book reviews and you may express your opinions on the themes, characters, or any other subject you want to talk about.

We want to thank you once more for taking the time to read our book. Your contributions are vital to us and will advance our writing. From the bottom of our hearts, thank you!

Matt Black

BONUS

1) HIIT Exercises

High-Intensity Interval Training (HIIT) is a good way to work out. It consists of short, intense intervals of exercise followed by rest or low-intensity action. It can help you lose fat, improve your heart health, and improve your mental health, among other things. HIIT is especially good for athletes, people who don't work out often, and people who are at risk for type 2 diabetes. It's a quick workout that works well and is good for people who don't have much time. But to avoid injury or burnout, you need a balanced plan that includes rest and other workouts.

DOWNLOAD IT RIGHT NOW!

https://tinyurl.com/mrxk9dn2

2) Free E-Book: Copycat Recipes By Matt Black

"Copycat Recipes" lets home cooks make popular American restaurant recipes. This cookbook includes breakfast and dessert recipes. It has a large number of KFC, Red Lobster, Cheesecake Factory, and Olive Garden-inspired recipes. Follow these recipes to impress your family and transport your dining table to these popular establishments. "Copycat Recipes" will inspire your inner chef and improve your home cooking.

DOWNLOAD IT RIGHT NOW!

https://tinyurl.com/4e9y8tsb

3) 10 SMOOTHIES RECIPES

Smoothies are blended beverages typically consisting of raw fruit, vegetables, and other ingredients such as dairy or ice. It utilizes the entire fruit or vegetable, which increases the fiber content and thus the digestive and satiating effects. Instead, juice is the liquid that remains after the pulp and other solids have been removed from fruits and vegetables. Consequently, smoothies give a more well-rounded nutritional profile than juices.

1. Banana Berry Smoothie

Ingredients:

- 1 ripe banana

- 1 cup mixed berries (fresh or frozen)

- 1 cup almond milk

Procedure:

1. Peel the banana and cut it into chunks.

2. Add all the ingredients to a blender and blend until smooth.

3. Serve immediately.

Calories: 200

Sugar: 28 g

2. Green Goddess Smoothie

Ingredients:

- 1 cup spinach

- 1 green apple

- 1 cup coconut water

Procedure:

1. Core the apple and cut it into chunks.

2. Add all the ingredients to a blender and blend until smooth.

3. Serve immediately.

Calories: 120

Sugar: 20 g

3. Tropical Delight Smoothie

Ingredients:

- 1 cup pineapple chunks
- 1 ripe banana
- 1 cup coconut milk

Procedure:

1. Peel the banana and cut it into chunks.

2. Add all the ingredients to a blender and blend until smooth.

3. Serve immediately.

Calories: 250

Sugar: 30 g

4. Peanut Butter Banana Smoothie

Ingredients:

- 1 ripe banana
- 2 tablespoons peanut butter
- 1 cup almond milk

Procedure:

1. Peel the banana and cut it into chunks.

2. Add all the ingredients to a blender and blend until smooth.

3. Serve immediately.

Calories: 300

Sugar: 15 g

5. Strawberry Banana Smoothie

Ingredients:

- 1 ripe banana

- 1 cup strawberries

- 1 cup almond milk

Procedure:

1. Peel the banana and cut it into chunks.

2. Add all the ingredients to a blender and blend until smooth.

3. Serve immediately.

Calories: 200

Sugar: 25 g

6. Mango Tango Smoothie

Ingredients:

- 1 ripe mango

- 1 ripe banana

- 1 cup coconut water

Procedure:

1. Peel the mango and banana and cut them into chunks.

2. Add all the ingredients to a blender and blend until smooth.

3. Serve immediately.

Calories: 250

Sugar: 40 g

7. Blueberry Bliss Smoothie

Ingredients:

- 1 cup blueberries

- 1 ripe banana

- 1 cup almond milk

Procedure:

1. Peel the banana and cut it into chunks.

2. Add all the ingredients to a blender and blend until smooth.

3. Serve immediately.

Calories: 200

Sugar: 25 g

8. Pineapple Paradise Smoothie

Ingredients:

- 1 cup pineapple chunks

- 1 cup coconut milk

Procedure:

1. Add all the ingredients to a blender and blend until smooth.

2. Serve immediately.

Calories: 200

Sugar: 25 g

9. Cherry Almond Smoothie

Ingredients:

- 1 cup cherries (pitted)

- 1 cup almond milk

Procedure:

1. Add all the ingredients to a blender and blend until smooth.

2. Serve immediately.

Calories: 150

Sugar: 20 g

10. Peachy Keen Smoothie

Ingredients:

- 1 ripe peach

- 1 ripe banana

- 1 cup almond milk

Procedure:

1. Peel the peach and banana and cut them into chunks.

2. Add all the ingredients to a blender and blend until smooth.

3. Serve immediately.

Calories: 200

Sugar: 30 g

Printed in Great Britain
by Amazon

28533716R00075